A Handbag

A play

Anthony Horowitz

Samuel French—London
www.samuelfrench-london.co.uk

Please see page iv for further copyright information

CHARACTERS

Rose also Lady Bracknell
George also Jack Worthing
Allan also Algernon Moncrieff
Specs also Algernon, Gwendolen, Jack, Cecily
Irene also Gwendolen
Kinsey also Lane

All the characters are aged between 18 and 22

A Handbag was originally commissioned by the Royal National Theatre as part of the New Connections season sponsored by the Royal National Theatre, London and the Bank of America.

NOTE

If the swearing in the play is a problem then Anthony Horowitz would prefer it to be softened at the director's discretion rather than for the play not to be performed at all.

CREDITS FOR PROGRAMMES

The following credits should appear in any programmes in connection with amateur productions:

A Handbag originally commissioned by the Royal National Theatre as part of New Connections season sponsored by the Royal National Theatre, London and the Bank of America

A HANDBAG

A stage

The scene is Algernon Moncrieff's flat in Half-Moon Street. The room is luxuriously and artistically furnished. Except it isn't

This is a dress rehearsal of The Importance of Being Earnest, *being performed in some sort of institution, somewhere. The characters might appear in nineteenth-century costume — or some sad stab at it*

And all but one of the characters have three names: their names in the play; the names that they call themselves; and their real names, which we will never discover

Rose (as Lady Bracknell) and George (as Jack Worthing) are on stage, performing part of Act I of The Importance of Being Earnest. *She is about nineteen and trying hard to grasp the world in which she finds herself. He is middle-class, articulate and seems to be in charge*

Rose (*as Lady Bracknell*) Now to minor matters. Are your parents living?
George (*as Jack Worthing*) I am afraid I really don't know. The fact is, Lady Bracknell, I said I had lost my parents. It would be nearer the truth to say that my parents have lost me … I don't actually know who I am by birth. I was … well, I was found.
Rose (*as Lady Bracknell*) Found?
George (*as Jack Worthing*) The late Mr Thomas Cardew, an old gentleman of a very charitable and kindly disposition, found me, and gave me the name of Worthing, because he happened to have a first-class ticket for Worthing in his pocket at the time. Worthing is a place in Sussex: it is a seaside resort.

Rose (*as Lady Bracknell*) Where did the charitable gentleman, who had a first-class ticket for this seaside resort, find you?

George (*as Jack Worthing*) In a handbag.

Rose (*as Lady Bracknell*) A handbag?

George (*Jack Worthing*) Yes, Lady Bracknell. I was in a handbag — a somewhat large, black-leather handbag with handles to it — an ordinary handbag, in fact.

Rose (*as Lady Bracknell*) In what locality did this Mr James, or Thomas, Cardew, come across this ordinary handbag?

George (*as Jack Worthing*) In the cloakroom at Victoria Station. It was given to him in mistake for his own.

Rose (*as Lady Bracknell*) The cloakroom at Victoria Station?

George (*as Jack Worthing*) Yes. The Brighton line.

Allan (Algernon Moncrieff) enters. Allan keeps his own council but he has a rough intelligence. He's largely self-taught … but it's left large gaps

Allan (*as Algernon Moncrieff*) Didn't it go off all right, old boy? You don't mean to say Gwendolen refused you? I know it is a way she has. She is always refusing people. I think it is most ill-natured of her.

A pause. Rose and George stare at Allan. He becomes aware that he's done something wrong

Allan What's wrong?

George What do you think?

Allan Tell me.

George No, Allan. Why don't you try to work it out?

Allan I got the right line …

George Did you?

Allan Yeah. It's the right line. Definitely. (*As Algernon*) Didn't it go off all right, old boy? You don't mean to say ——

George (*interrupting*) It's the right line.

Rose The Brighton line.

Allan What then?

George Take a look at me. And just think for a minute. Am I alone?

Allan Alone in what sense?

George You're a twat, Allan.

Rose You shouldn't call him that.

George (*to Allan*) I'm with her. I'm in the middle of the scene. I'm still talking.

Rose You shouldn't use aggressive language. You know what it is? It's verbal bullying.

Allan So ...?

George So, obviously, you've come on too soon.

Rose It's inappropriate behaviour.

George Rose. What are you going on about?

Rose You called him a twat.

George He is a twat. He came on a page too early.

Allan I come on at the end of the scene with Lady Bracknell.

George That's the point I'm trying to make. It's obvious I'm still talking to Lady Bracknell. I mean, there she is! Look at her! She's standing next to me. The scene hasn't ended.

Rose (*as Lady Bracknell*) The line is immaterial, Mr Worthing …

George Not now, Rose. (*To Allan*) Weren't you listening?

Allan Do you want the honest truth here?

George You weren't listening.

Allan I was listening … after a fashion. But I wasn't really following. I was what you might call half listening.

George Am I half stupid or are you doing this on purpose? You come on too early. You come on too late. Sometimes you don't come on at all. It seems to depend on the weather … or what mood you're in. I don't know! I mean, you're new here, Allan. I'll grant you that. Relatively new. Maybe I haven't quite worked you out. But tell me. A simple yes or no. Are you deliberately undermining me? Have you got something against me?

Allan You're getting very worked up about this.

George Have you got something against me?

Allan No.

George Because if you have, you can tell me.

Allan I've got nothing against you, George.

George Would you have preferred someone else to be the director?

Allan I can't think of a better director.

George Then, as director, can I remind you that we're going to be performing this play in front of an audience — a real audience, a live audience — one week from now? We've got the stage. We've got the seats. We've sold the tickets.

Rose We haven't sold any tickets.

George All right. We've given the tickets away. But they've still said they'll come — that's the same thing. They're expecting a performance. (*To Allan*) And you seem to have set out to deliberately sabotage it.

Allan I came on a few lines early. My attention was wandering, that's all. Specs should have told me. He normally gives me my cue.

George Normally.

Allan In so far as anything about Specs is normal, yes.

George And where was Specs?

Allan He was there. (*Pointing*) He was there …

George What was he doing?

Allan He was doing what he always does … at least, when the lights are on. He was reading. He had his head in a book.

George Which book? (*Pause*) The book of the play?

Allan Obviously.

George He was reading the lines?

Allan Yes.

George Did he know what was going on?

Allan I suppose so. Why don't you ask him?

George I will ask him. I'll ask him now. (*Calling*) Specs!

Specs doesn't come

Rose He's not coming.

George Give him time.

Specs still doesn't come. Everyone is looking off stage

Allan We could be here all week.

George You just have to be patient.

Allan He's not moving.

George He's got slow reactions.

Allan Well, it's your rehearsal. But I should just point out that, at this rate, we're not even going to get to the next scene.

George (*losing it*) Specs! Will you get out here!

At last Specs arrives. He is in charge of prompting and carries an ancient, hard-cover edition of the play with loose pages. He is not in costume. His glasses are hideously thick, distorting his eyes. Specs is a mess. He has a terrible stammer. But when he reads from books, he can speak normally

Specs Yes, George?

Rose Look at him. You've frightened him. He's shaking like a leaf.

Allan None of the leaves in this place ever shake.

Rose That's because they're made out of plastic. It's a Health and Safety measure.

Allan I've never felt healthy here. Or particularly safe.

Rose Come here, Specs. I'll look after you.

Allan Physical contact isn't allowed.

Rose I'm offering him proximity. It's not the same.

George Specs. Listen to me. No one's going to hurt you. There's just one thing I want to know. Are you looking after Allan?

Specs Yes, George.

George But you didn't give him his cue.

Specs No.

George Why didn't you give him his cue?

Specs Because it wasn't the right time.

George That's a good answer. That's the right answer. (*To Allan*) He couldn't give you the cue because it wasn't your cue. So why are you trying to blame him?

Allan I'm not trying to blame anyone.

George Specs has been here longer than any of us. Specs knows what he's doing. You just have to trust him.

Allan I do trust him.

George You think he's dysfunctional.

Allan I never said that.

George He is dysfunctional. He's got a certificate to prove it. But he knows what he's doing. And he's body and soul behind this play. Aren't you, Specs?

Specs tries to speak but can't articulate

Allan Out of interest, and with all respect, why did you choose him to be the prompter?

George I didn't choose him. He volunteered.

Allan He could have played Algernon. He could still play Algernon. He knows all the lines. And — correct me if I've got this wrong but — he's got this stammer when he talks but he doesn't stammer when he reads, so wouldn't he be better out here performing?

George That's not possible.

Allan Why not?

George He gets stage fright.

Allan He's scared of a lot of things.

George That's true. But he's not had an easy life. He was bullied when he was young.

Allan We were all bullied when we were young.

George Yeah — but for him it started in the maternity ward. His mother rejected him. Even the nurses didn't want to know. The other babies used to gang up on him and steal his pacifier. Nineteen years later and his mother's still got post-natal depression. You can't blame her. The only friends he's ever had have been in this place and we don't much like him either.

Rose I think he's all right.

George Rose, there's nothing all right about Specs. Why are you pretending otherwise?

Rose I'm just trying to be kind.

George If you want to be kind, you'll get back to the scene and let him get back to the wings. That's what he likes. It's being out of sight, isn't it, Specs?

Specs Yes, George.

George Right then. Shall we take it from the top?

Allan Do we have to?

George OK. We'll take it from the middle.

Allan Suppose we take it from where we left off?

Rose Wait a minute. Wait a minute …

George What is it now, Rose?

Rose Can I ask you something?

George Can't it wait?

Rose No. It's something I don't understand.

George (*exasperated*) Go on.

Rose It's about this handbag.

George The handbag.

Rose Yes.

George What about it?

Rose I was just wondering how big it was. I mean, how would you fit in?

George Well, it was a big handbag. In those days, women had big handbags.

Rose Those days.

George When the play was written.

Rose When was that?

George I don't know. Ask Specs. He was the one who found it.

Rose Specs?

Specs Eighteen nine— (*His stammer is so bad, he can't finish the date*)

George (*interrupting*) It doesn't matter when it was written. It was a long time ago.

Allan And it's by Oscar Wilde.

George (*pleasantly surprised*) That's right.

Allan He wore a green carnation. He was Irish. He wrote plays. And he was queer.

Rose He wasn't a queer. He was gay. There's nothing wrong with that.

Allan I know his sort.

Rose There's no need for negative stereotyping.

Allan His name was Oscar Wilde and he liked boys. He liked working-class boys. He took them back to his place and he took advantage of them. What am I supposed to call him?

Rose A homosexual. From the Greek.

Allan From the Greek … what? What he did or what he called it?

Specs Both.

Allan It makes me sick. If you ask me, they shouldn't have allowed him out to write comedies. They should have put him in jail.

Specs They — (*Trying to tell Allan that they did*)

Allan (*angry*) What, Specs?

Specs Never mind.

George Getting back to your entrance, Allan …

Rose Wait a minute. You haven't answered my question. I don't see how you could have got into the handbag, no matter how big it was. Maybe if it was a suitcase …!

George What?

Rose And even then, they'd never have been able to carry you.

George works out what's going on

George Rose. You haven't understood a single word of this play. Have you?

Rose Yes, I have.

George No, you haven't. When I'm found in the handbag, I'm a baby. That's the whole point. I'm not big. I'm small. I'm a baby.

Rose A baby.

George Yes.

Rose How old?

George I don't know. A couple of months.

Rose Is the handbag done up?

George I don't know.

Rose Because if it's done up, it could be very dangerous. You could suffocate.

Allan That's true.

George Well, obviously I haven't suffocated because if I'd suffocated I wouldn't be here and there wouldn't be any play.

Rose Even so … it would be a horrible thing to do, to put a baby into a handbag, to seal it up and leave it in the dark. It would be so scared and it wouldn't be able to breathe. And then to leave it in a railway station, on its own. How could anyone do that?

George It's a comedy!

Allan Oscar Wilde, knocking up little kids. It's not witty. It's repulsive.

Rose I've got funny lines.

Allan Have you?

Rose Yes.

Allan Tell me one funny line.

Rose What … now?

Allan Tell me one funny line.

Rose Well …

Allan Come on, Rose.

Rose Wait …

Allan There aren't any.

George There are lots.

Rose (*bursting out as Lady Bracknell*) To be born, or at any rate, bred in a handbag, whether it had handles or not, seems to me to display a contempt for the ordinary decencies of life that reminds one of the worst excesses of the French Revolution.

A pause. Nobody laughs

George There you are! That was great!

Allan You thought that was funny?

George Yes.

Allan You're not laughing.

George Well, I've heard it before.

Allan It wasn't funny.

George It was out of context.

Allan OK, Rose, you tell me. Since you're the one falling about with mirth, what's so funny about that line?

Rose I think it's funny that she's got bread in the handbag.

Allan Bread in the handbag? You think she's got a loaf of bread in the handbag? She hasn't got anything in her handbag.

Rose She's got a baby.

Allan You don't get any of it, do you. You don't understand a single word! What about the French Revolution? What was that about?

Rose Why are you picking on me? I never learned dancing. I don't know …

Allan I'm not picking on you. I'm with you. I don't get it either. I don't even get the plot.

George It couldn't be simpler. It's a comedy.

Allan So what's it about?

George You want to know what it's about.

Allan That's what I said.

George Well, it's obvious. Specs! You tell him …

Specs (*fluently*) The play may be superficial but relishes it, a triumph of surface over substance, a distillation of theatre that ultimately defines theatre itself. Here — appearance, style and narrative are treated as essence not just by the protagonists but by the author whose voice, a *deus ex machina*, binds the action in a totality that is unmistakably his.

Allan Where did you get that from?

Specs (*miserably*) The introduction.

Allan The introduction. (*Pause*) Did you understand what you just said?

Specs No.

Allan A *deus ex machina*. What's that?

Rose A day in a machine. (*Realizing*) It's like being here!

Allan Come on, Specs. Why don't you explain it to me? Why don't you just tell me the story?

George If you ask Specs to elaborate, we'll be here all night.

Allan Then you tell me.

George The story.

Allan What's it about?

George The story.

Allan Yes.

George You ought to know it by now.

Allan I do know it. I just want to hear it from you.

George Right. (*Pause*) I'm Jack Worthing. All right? Jack. I have a fake brother called Ernest who doesn't exist and that's the name I also call myself. Sometimes I'm Jack. Sometimes I'm Ernest. You're my best friend and your name is Algy. And you're a real friend. Someone I can trust. Not someone who'd lead me to do something that I'd regret for the rest of my life. And I'm in love. I'm in love with your cousin, Gwendolen, who's really nice and not a slut, but she doesn't like me as Jack, she likes me as Ernest. You're in love with Cecily who's also a nice girl, like Gwendolen, but you also call yourself Ernest and Cecily has always dreamed that she'll meet someone called Ernest so she falls in love with you. Lady Bracknell is your aunt with the funny lines which are funny if they're delivered properly and she's also Gwendolen's mother and she doesn't want me to marry Gwendolen, and I'm Cecily's gardener and I don't want her to marry you.

Allan I'm not sure I'm any the wiser.

Specs Not gardener.

Rose What about the handbag?

George What?

Specs Guardian.

George What about the handbag, Rose? It's leather with long straps.

Allan Well, I'm glad that's sorted.

George Right. So now — can we get started? Are you ready to make your entrance?

Allan Absolutely.

George Specs — give him his cue.

Specs opens the play and reads out the cue without stammering

Specs (*reading*) Algernon, from the other room, strikes up the "Wedding March". Jack looks perfectly furious and goes to the door: "For goodness sake don't play that ghastly tune, Algy! How idiotic you are." The music stops and Algernon enters cheerily

George Thank you.

Specs That's — (*He can't finish the sentence*)

George Now get lost.

Specs leaves

So, I think we get it now, Allan. We hear you playing the piano and then you come in.

Allan Playing the piano.

George No. You stop playing the piano and then you come in. Otherwise you'd look pretty stupid, wouldn't you?

Rose We did all this yesterday.

George And the day before. (*To Allan*) How can you have forgotten? You wait for the music. Do you want to hear it?

Allan (*calling*) Specs!

From off stage comes the sound of a wedding march, played on a xylophone

Rose That's not a piano.

George I know it's not a piano. We don't have a piano here.

Rose (*nodding, in explanation*) Pianos have got piano wire.

Allan That makes complete sense.

George I don't think it really matters. All that matters is that I hear a musical instrument being played . . .

Rose It could be a trombone.

George It could be anything. And I call out. (*As Jack Worthing*) For goodness' sake don't play that ghastly tune, Algy. The music stops.

It stops. And then . . .

Allan (*as Algernon*) Didn't it go off all right, old boy? You don't mean to say Gwendolen refused you?

George Right. That was excellent. That was perfect. I really think we're getting somewhere.

Rose About this handbag . . .

George Rose . . . we've done all that.

Rose No. There's something else.

George What is it?

Rose Why does the handbag have to be leather?

George Oh God.

Rose Why is it leather?

George Do you really want to know?

Rose Yeah.

George Do you have to know?

A pause. George searches for the answer

It's just written that way.
Rose You could change the line.
George You can't change the lines!
Rose Why not?
George Because it's Oscar Wilde. If you changed the lines, it wouldn't be funny any more.
Rose Why can't it be a plastic handbag?
George They didn't have plastic handbags when the play was written.
Rose Why not?
George It wasn't in fashion. Nobody wore plastic. In society, nobody would have been seen dead wearing plastic, not even dead people. It just wasn't the thing.
Rose I just think we ought to think about the cow.
George What cow?
Rose The cow that made the handbag. Why should an animal have to die just to make a fashion accessory?
George Look … this is *The Importance of Being Earnest*. Not *The Importance of Being a Vegetarian*. I mean, we've been rehearsing it for weeks …
Allan Months.
George Isn't it a bit late to be bringing it up now?

Two more characters enter. Irene, who plays Gwendolen, is a very tough Glaswegian girl. Not attractive. Kinsey, who plays Lane (the butler) has a similar background to George. In fact the two of them grew up together

Irene For Christ's sake, George.
George Irene …
Irene What's happening?
George We're getting there.

Irene What are you doing?

George We've got a problem with the scene. Nothing to worry about. We're sorting it.

Irene You've been sorting it for a very long time.

George We're working on it.

Irene How long am I supposed to wait out there?

George Two pages. Two minutes a page. Four minutes.

Kinsey You can tell he's the one with the maths GCSE.

George Just wait another four minutes. We've got a hitch.

Irene I'm fed up waiting. I've been waiting all fucking day. I've just been sitting there, fucking waiting.

Kinsey She's angry.

George I can see that.

Irene I'm angry.

Rose You're not meant to be angry, Irene. That's why they send us to anger management.

Irene Actually, anger management really pisses me off. You need anger to live in this place.

Rose What's wrong with this place? I like it here.

Irene No you don't, Rose. They fill you with pills. You only think you like it.

Rose It's the same thing.

Irene What?

Rose Thinking I like it. And liking it. What's the difference?

Irene The difference is that it's a fucking hallucination.

Rose I like the hallucination.

Irene That's what's wrong with this place. Don't you see? Are you so thick you don't see it? Every day they're trying to turn us into something we're not.

George Do we have to have this conversation now?

Kinsey (*ignoring him*) You've got it wrong, Irene. They're untying the knots and they're trying to turn us into something.

Irene That's very clever, Kinsey. You really fancy yourself, don't you? Anyone would think you'd had an education.

Kinsey I've had a re-education.

Irene It's not the same thing.

Allan She's got a point.

Rose At least he isn't self-harming.

Kinsey No. I let other people do that for me.

Irene Are you having a go at me, Rose?

Rose No. I wouldn't do that.

Irene Because if you're having a go at me, we can step outside.

Kinsey You haven't stepped outside in eleven years.

Irene But one day I will — and you'll be the first person I'll meet there.

Kinsey I'm not going anywhere.

Irene I'll tell you what I hate about this place. They're trying to patch us together with their medicine and their methods. But I'm not going to let them do it to me.

Kinsey You like being a total screw-up.

Irene Fuck you, Kinsey …

Rose I don't like that sort of language. It's wrong.

Irene (*continuing*) If you're so clever, how did you end up here? How did you even end up being called Kinsey? It's not your name.

Kinsey It is my name.

Irene It's the name that they gave you. But it wasn't the one you were born with. Not the one your parents gave you.

Kinsey I lost my parents.

Irene You mean your parents lost you. And as quickly as they could.

George Irene …

Irene (*to George*) What was it that the newspapers called the two of you, George? You and Kinsey? Do you want to remind me?

Rose We never talk about that. You know we're not meant to talk about that.

Irene They had a name for you too, Rose.

Rose They didn't know me.

Irene They knew what you did. After that, they didn't *want* to know you. Nobody did. They still don't.

Rose One day I'll be out of here and I'll tell them the truth.

Irene Just make sure they haven't eaten.

George Why don't we get back to the play?

Allan We were talking about the handbag.

George sees this as a way of getting back into the rehearsal

George That's right. Rose asked about the handbag. Rose? I think you had an interesting point.

Rose I don't see why it can't be plastic.

Irene Oh Jesus!

George (*to Irene*) Can I answer her?

Irene Go ahead.

George It's an interesting point, Rose. But the baby would die in a plastic handbag. It wouldn't be able to breathe. Even if the handbag was open, its little lips would get stuck to the side and that would be the end of it. You don't want to put a baby in a plastic handbag. It has to be leather. All right?

Allan You know, the more I think about it, the more I wonder if this is the right play …

George That's because you don't understand the plot.

Allan So maybe you can help me.

George I've already done that. I've told you.

Allan You didn't tell me what happens at the end.

George (*thrown*) What?

Allan The end. What happens at the end?

George Why are you asking that?

Allan Because I want to know.

George You've never asked before.

Allan I'm asking now.

George You know perfectly well. We don't know what happens at the end. We don't have the last pages.

Allan We've lost some pages.

George Yes.

Irene How many pages?

George Act Three.

Allan We don't have Act Three?

George No.

Allan None of it?

George No.

Irene Fuck.

Kinsey I thought it all ended a bit abruptly.

Allan What happened to Act Three?

George It fell out. When they removed the staples, some of the pages fell out.

Allan Quite a lot of pages.

George Yes.

Rose We're not allowed staples. None of the books have any staples. They're pointy and they're made of metal so they take them out.

Irene Stupid bastards.

Allan So what happened to the pages?

George We looked for them but we couldn't find them.

Allan Doesn't that somewhat defeat the purpose?

George No. It doesn't matter what happens in the end. Oscar Wilde didn't work that way. He just wanted you to have a good time. And when you're having a good time, you don't want it to end.

Rose I think they live happily ever after. They get married and they have their own place to live and a job … and maybe one of those new Minis with leather seats and a sun roof.

Allan And they go down the boozer Friday nights, get pissed, get into punch-ups and vomit over the kerb?

Rose It sounds lovely.

Allan I'm beginning to wonder if performing this play is really such a good idea. I mean, think of the audience. What are we going to do when halfway through ——

George Two-thirds.

Allan —— two thirds of the way, we just stop.

George They'll forgive us.

Kinsey That'll make a change.

Allan The play is an antique. The jokes don't work. It's missing half the pages. And it was written by a pervert.

George Anything else?

Allan Well, yes. Since you mention it. I don't think it's relevant.

George Relevant? Who says it has to be relevant?

Allan Well, it might help. It might make the experience more enjoyable. So tell me, George. Your starter for ten. *The Importance of Being Earnest.* What's the connection? To us.

Rose That's a good question.

Allan Because I'll tell you something. It certainly isn't cucumber sandwiches and girls called Gwendolen and marriages and handbags.

George It's a masterpiece! It's a much-loved English classic!

Kinsey By an Irishman.

George Don't start that again.

Allan I wouldn't go and see it. Who does? Can you tell me that? What's the actual point?

George It's simple, Allan. People love it.

Allan The play?

George The theatre. They love it. It doesn't matter what's on. Chekhov. Stendhal. Andrew Lloyd Webber. Going to the theatre … it's a big deal. Mums and dads, they get a babysitter for the kids ——

Rose (*alarmed*) Babysitters.

George —— and they go off together up to London's West End. There are loads of theatres all in a row and everyone dresses up. They're shown where to park by a kindly traffic warden and in they go in their suit and tie, programme, box of Black Magic, and then the lights go down and suddenly it's like they're in a different world. Algernon Moncrieff's flat in Half-Moon Street. The room is luxuriously and artistically furnished. The sound of a xylophone is heard in the adjoining room.

Rose A piano.

George It depends on the production.

Allan And people pay for this?

George It's culture. Of course they pay for it. A good seat in the stalls can cost fifteen quid and you may still have to put another ten pence in for a pair of binoculars — but they don't mind. It's worth it.

Allan I wouldn't go if you paid me.

Irene Yes, you would.

Allan Yes, I would. But I wouldn't enjoy it.

George You'd love it. A quick gin and tonic at the interval, served in the comfort of the crush bar, then the second half ——

Kinsey — three if you've got the whole play ——

George — applause, encore, lights up and out for dinner at your local Aberdeen Steak House, three courses served with a fine wine. That's what it's all about. That's an evening out.

Irene It's still a rubbish play. If I met someone like Gwendolen I'd want to nut her.

Rose You shouldn't say that.

Irene Oh give it a break, Rose. Have you got anything to say that doesn't come out of the rule book?

Rose The rule book is there for a reason.

Irene Gwendolen makes me want to throw up. She wouldn't have lasted two minutes on my estate. She'd have been killed just for her name.

Allan You still haven't answered my question, George. Why did you choose this play?

George All right. I'll tell you. There were two plays in the library. *The Importance of Being Earnest* and *Julius Caesar* and if you think this one is irrelevant, you should have read the other one. It was full of Romans.

Rose My mum went to Rome.

George Ancient Romans. In togas and things.

Allan Did it have any jokes?

George No. But it had a murder.

Rose We don't want to do that sort of play here.

Allan Who got murdered?

George Julius Caesar. They stabbed him over and over.

Irene That sounds more like it.

Allan Why?

George It was very complicated. They didn't like him.

Allan Was it a gang?

George Yes. A gang. With knives. They wait for him in the market and then they do him over.

Rose You mean … like a video nasty?

George It is a bit like that.

Rose Not suitable.

George I wouldn't have said so.

Allan Julius Caesar. I can't say I ever saw it. And I used to watch a lot of video nasties …

George You know, I'm not sure …

George is about to explain the nature of Julius Caesar. He is interrupted

Allan I used to watch them all the time. When I was a kid. I lived down the road from my local Blockbuster and the manager took a shine to me. He used to take me into the back room to show me these dirty films, not that you get very dirty films at Blockbuster. Smutty more like, though still capable of affecting an impressionable mind.

Irene It was porn.

Allan I preferred the action films. *Die Hard. Scream Two.* Little did I know that they might one day furnish me with the title of my own autobiography. But the best news was when Blockbuster started renting computer games. Now I could enjoy the violence in the privacy of my own room.

Rose *Zelda: Warrior Princess.*

Allan I preferred *Doom* and Lara Croft. They were great. I mean, the graphics were really in your face. Only my stepdad … he was dead against them. He used to go on and on about them. All the shooting. All the killing. People getting mauled by lions and sliced up by monsters …

Kinsey You couldn't make a computer game of *The Importance of Being Earnest.* I mean … you could. But who'd want to play it? Eat another fucking cucumber sandwich and advance to the next level. It would never work.

Allan My stepdad used to say that one thing would only lead to another. The blood-splatter and the sound effects. They made it more and more realistic until in the end it almost felt like the real thing and who could blame you if you decided that you wanted … you know … if you wouldn't actually prefer the real thing. It was only one small step.

Irene Are you saying you're here because of computer games?

Allan No. I'm not saying that. My stepdad didn't want me to play violent games. He used to search me every time I came back from school. I had a PlayStation but he personally chose all the software. *Civilization. The Sims.* Stuff like that. He'd search my room … he was worried about my long-term development. Anyway, one night he came in unexpectedly and caught me red-handed. I'd just managed to get my hands on *Grand Theft Auto* and there I was blasting away, left right and centre. And there he was, standing at the door.

Rose What did he do?

Allan He beat me up. Put me in hospital for two days.

Rose Was that when you ran away?

Allan I wouldn't even have been able to walk away after that. I could only just about manage to limp to school. I ran away three months later, as soon as I was able.

Rose To London.

Allan Yeah.

Rose What's London like?

Allan London?

Rose Yeah.

Allan It's big.

Rose It's got pigeons. And the Millennium Wheel. I'd love to go on the Millennium Wheel.

Irene What's the point of going on the fucking Millennium Wheel? It'll only take you back where you started.

Allan I was labouring under the mistaken belief that the streets of London would be lined with gold. But they weren't. The streets were lined with creeps and weirdos.

Rose Where did you sleep?

Allan That was difficult. The police were always moving you on. I was only eighteen. In the end, I found a place near Victoria Station.

Kinsey Victoria Station. Well, well, well. Maybe there's a connection after all.

Rose The handbag! It was left in the cloakroom at Victoria Station.

Allan I got to know the station very well after I came to London. I was found by a great many gentlemen of a charitable and kindly disposition and many of them did, indeed, take me to the cloakroom.

George We don't want to know about this.

Irene I do!

George It's not relevant.

Allan It's the play that's not relevant. I vote we don't do it.

George What?

Allan Let's take a vote on it. I say we junk it.

George But we've been working on it for months.

Irene I don't care. I think he's right.

George We can't have a vote. Half the cast isn't here.

Allan That is their vote, George. They're not here because, all in all,
   they'd prefer to be on medication. That's their commitment.
Kinsey We're all committed.
George If we had a vote, I'd win. I want to do it. Specs wants to do it.
   Kinsey wants to do it. Rose wants to do it.
Irene I don't want to do it.
George That just leaves two of you.
Allan Specs doesn't want to do it.
George Yes, he does.
Irene Then let's hear him say it.
George You want to hear him say it?
Irene Yes.
George (*calling*) Specs!
Allan Here we go again.

A pause. They wait for Specs

Kinsey Anyone fancy a game of Scrabble while we're waiting?
Irene I hate fucking Scrabble.
Kinsey I can't understand why. You're so good with the four-letter
   words.

Specs appears

Specs Yes, George?
George Yes or no, Specs. Do you want to do this play? Feel free to
   nod.

Specs nods

George There you are.
Allan You haven't thought this through, George. It's a terrible play. It's a
   horrible play. We're all going to make complete idiots of ourselves.
George No, Allan. You're the one who doesn't see it. When it's done
   properly, it's a brilliant play. It's hilarious.
Allan When it's done properly …

George We just haven't got there yet. That's what we're working towards. I can show you. I can show you. Do it, Specs.

Specs Me?

George Show them. (*To the others*) Sit down. Watch him. This is how it's done.

George, Kinsey, Allan, Rose and Irene sit down. Specs is centre stage

Right.

A pause. Then, unexpectedly, Specs provides a faultless, virtuoso performance, acting all the parts at high speed, changing voice and character, making the play live

Specs (*as Cecily*) Here is Ernest. (*As Algernon*) My own love. (*He offers to kiss her. As Cecily*) A moment, Ernest. May I ask you — are you engaged to be married to this young lady? (*As Algernon*) Of course not! What could have put such an idea into your pretty little head? (*As Cecily*) Thank you. (*Presenting her cheek to be kissed*) You may.

Specs as Algernon kisses Specs as Cecily

(*As Gwendolen*) I felt there was some slight error, Miss Cardew. The gentleman who is now embracing you is my cousin, Mr Algernon Moncrieff.

Specs as Cecily breaks away from Specs as Algernon

(*As Algernon*) Oh! (*As Cecily*) Are you called Algernon? (*As Algernon*) I cannot deny it. (*As Cecily*) Oh! (*As Gwendolen*) Is your name really John? (*As Jack*) I could deny it if I liked. I could deny anything if I liked. But my name certainly is John. It has been John for years. (*As Cecily to Gwendolen*) A gross deception has been practised on both of us. (*As Gwendolen*) My poor wounded Cecily. (*As Cecily*) My sweet wronged Gwendolen. (*As Gwendolen*) You will call me sister, will you not?

Cecily and Gwendolen embrace each other. Specs does this by embracing himself

George There you are. He's astonishing. He's a virtuoso.

Kinsey Maybe he should do it as a one-man show.

George Don't you start, Kinsey. We're not doing it as a one-man show but we are doing it. That's been decided. So now get off stage and let's get back to the first scene.

Kinsey Wait a minute. Wait a minute. You never gave me a vote.

George You did get a vote. You voted to do it.

Kinsey No, George. This was all your idea. I did it because you told me to.

George That's not true. That's not me. I wouldn't do that.

Kinsey You made the decision, George.

George No.

Kinsey Well, I've changed my mind. I don't want to do it. I'm voting against it.

Rose I can't keep up with this.

Irene It's a draw. Three all. I'm going to bed.

George Wait! What do you want, Kinsey?

Kinsey Well, I wouldn't have minded a decent part, for a start. I'm the butler. I just bring on the muffins and the cucumber sandwiches. And they don't even exist. It's embarrassing.

George They're imaginary. They're imaginary cucumber sandwiches. That's part of the drama.

Rose Are they in triangles?

Kinsey Rose …

Rose Or little squares? That's how I used to do them. Natty used to love them. We'd go down to the bottom of the garden and we'd have a little picnic in the daisies. Little Natty and me. We'd have little, tiny cups of tea out of a doll's house cup and I made sure the water was never scalding hot or anything like that. I put the knife away. That's why I wanted to do this play. Because it reminded me of the picnics … the cucumber sandwiches. And when I imagine them, they're always cut into squares.

Kinsey (*to George*) You see what I mean? This is total bullshit.

Irene I'm with you there.

Allan That's it, then. Three against three. That's not good enough.

Irene The end. Curtain. Fuck off.

George Wait a minute. Wait a minute. Kinsey, let me talk to you about this.

Kinsey We've talked enough, George.

George Just the two of us. Alone. You and me.

Kinsey You and me?

George Like we used to be. Just for a moment.

Kinsey You want to talk.

George Yes.

Kinsey I can do that.

George Thank you, Kinsey. (*He turns to the rest of them*) All right, everyone? Did you get that? We're going to take five.

Rose Five what?

George Five minutes, Rose. It's a technical term.

Kinsey Five minutes alone.

George One on one.

Rose doesn't understand this either

Please.

Irene, Rose, Specs and Allan leave

Allan (*as he goes, muttering to Kinsey*) You tell him …

Kinsey and George are alone. A pause

George Why are you doing this? What do you want?

Another pause. Kinsey is savouring the moment. He has the upper hand

Kinsey Let's talk about motivation.

George What?

Kinsey I think you heard me, George. You never gave me any time during rehearsals. So let's talk about motivation.

George Now?

Kinsey That's right.

George Your character is a butler, Kinsey. He doesn't have motivation. He gets paid, which is the next best thing.

Kinsey That's not what I mean. That's not what I had in mind.

George What then?

Kinsey I'd be interested in your motivation for casting me.

George Casting you?

Kinsey As the butler. As Lane.

George You want a bigger part.

Kinsey I don't want any part at all. But since Allan is complete crap and doesn't want to do this and keeps coming on at the wrong time, I would like to know, just out of interest, why you didn't cast me as Algernon.

George You weren't right for Algernon.

Kinsey You think Rose is right for Lady Bracknell?

George There's nothing wrong with Rose.

Kinsey Lady Bracknell is a respectable, witty doyenne of Victorian society. Rose is completely thick.

George It's a different interpretation.

Kinsey I should have played Algernon. Algernon and Jack are lifelong friends.

George That's why you're wrong for the part.

Kinsey Ah. (*Pause*) I could have acted.

George I couldn't.

Kinsey It would have been nice, a bit of comic banter between us.

George It wouldn't work.

Kinsey You didn't want to give it a try?

George Not any more.

Kinsey I was the best friend you ever had, George.

George That's what I thought, once. But you led me right up the garden path.

Kinsey We went up the garden path together.

George But it wasn't a garden path, was it? It led us here. Unless this is the only garden in the country where they put the hydrangeas behind razor-wire.

Kinsey You still blame me. (*A long pause*) How much of it do you really remember? It was a long time ago. Do you ever think about Ashurst?

George Not if I can help it.

Kinsey You and me. We were inseparable. Same school. Same street. Same brand of cigarette. You remember that? Ten Marlboro Lite from old Mr Harris on the corner? You get his attention, I nick 'em. And the ice-cream van. The chime of the bells on a hot summer day. Running in front of it to see if we could fake an insurance claim. And going up the garden path, since you mention it. Breaking into the conservatory.

George You were a year older than me.

Kinsey But you were the smart one. The director. You remember the bicycle rides? Ashurst. Findon. And then down the A24 to Worthing.

George I don't want to talk about Worthing.

Kinsey And then, of course, you must remember coming here …

George I remember that.

Kinsey I never thought they'd send us to the same place. Do you ever wonder why they did that? Perhaps it was therapy.

George Or punishment.

Kinsey I was twelve when I came here. I didn't understand what was happening. I didn't understand any of it. I remember they unlocked this door. We went in and they locked it behind us. And right in front of us there was another door. They unlocked it, we went through and then they locked it behind us. We came to a third door. Unlock, go through, lock it again. And then — I couldn't believe it — there was another door. "What's this?" I asked. "This is the front door," they said. That was when I knew I was in trouble. (*Pause*) Do you think they'll ever open those doors again, George? Is that your motivation? Be a good boy, put on a play, they'll look at you in a new light and let you out?

A pause

George They might.

Kinsey They won't.

George I'm different now.

Kinsey New name. New number. Same old George.

George No.

Kinsey Still trying to blame me.

George It was your idea.

Kinsey You're never going to leave here. You should be glad.

George No.

Kinsey Because you know what would happen if you walked through all those doors? There'd be a crowd waiting for you outside. All the journalists and photographers. They'd snap you. They'd snap you in half ...

George They've forgotten me.

Kinsey No one will ever forget you.

George They've forgiven me.

Kinsey You think so? Personally, I've never thought of journalists as the forgiving sort. And then there are the parents and the relatives, lining up to give you a good kicking. And then, waiting patiently in line, the rest of the world. "You're slime. You're evil." They'd rather you didn't exist.

George They don't know me. I've changed. And when I get out of here, I'll be someone else.

Kinsey The face of Satan.

George It was red-eye. That was all.

Kinsey A lethal injection, George. You remember that? Free with the *Daily Mail*. See page two, three, four, five, nine, ten, sixteen. They were even trying to kill you on the sports pages.

George I was eleven years old!

Kinsey That's no excuse.

George One day, they'll let us go.

Kinsey You think so? And what about the rest of them ... the rest of your cast? You really think they're going to let Rose out? Give her a job in a crèche, perhaps. Count Dracula to supply the character reference. Or Irene. Let her go back to her family — or what's left of them — in Glasgow. Allan. Specs. There are two people who'd be much happier walking the streets and I'm sure the streets would be much happier having them. Do you really see it happening? Don't you see what you are?

George Have you finished?

Kinsey Not really.

George The bell will be going.

Kinsey Well, no one else is.

George I want to go on with the rehearsal. I need your vote.

Kinsey And I need you, George. I need you.

A pause. George waits to see if Kinsey will object. He doesn't

George (*calling*) Allan. Irene. Rose. Specs.

Allan, Irene, Rose and Specs come back

We've had a discussion. We've hammered a few things out.

Rose (*urgently*) It wasn't my hammer!

George We've decided … we've put a lot of work into this. We all have. So we're going to continue.

Irene Shit.

Allan Kinsey, you're a wanker.

George So that's it, then. The decision has been made.

Kinsey Whose decision?

The moment of truth for George

George Kinsey wants to continue. Don't you, Kinsey. (*Pause. Then, to Kinsey*) Colin?

Kinsey What did you call me?

Rose Colin.

Irene Is that your name?

Kinsey It was my name. In Worthing.

Rose That's not allowed.

A pause. Then back to business

Kinsey Maybe he's right. We've got nothing else to do.

Allan OK. Just tell me one thing.

George What?

Allan Why are we doing this? Why are we bothering?

Irene Yeah — because frankly, between you and me, I can't think of a fucking reason.

George How can you ask this now, after all this time? We've got the costumes. We've got the set. You've learned your lines ... many of them in the right order. We've spent weeks. Months. How can you ask this now?

Allan Better late than never.

Irene I still say we stop. I still say we pack the whole thing in.

George No! We've voted.

Rose I might have changed my mind.

George What? (*He turns to Irene*) Have you talked to her?

Rose I don't know. I think it's a good idea.

George (*to the others*) There you are!

Rose But a lot of the things I think are good ideas turn out to be not good ideas after all. That's the trouble. Like the time with me and Natty. I thought it was a good idea but that's how I ended up here and if there's one thing I've learned, it's not to have good ideas.

Allan So you're against it.

George No. She's for it.

Rose No. I'm against it.

George She doesn't know what she's saying. She doesn't understand a single word that comes out of her lips.

Allan Then her vote doesn't count. She's disqualified.

Rose Let's talk about this tomorrow!

Irene Let's pack it in now.

George No. Wait. You don't see the importance. You don't see — one more week — how it could be. Listen to me. In a week's time, we'll have an audience. They'll come in through that door — and the door behind it — and they'll sit down and they'll watch us. And just for an hour, an hour and a half, they'll enjoy what we do. They'll see us eat the cucumber sandwiches and the muffins and they'll laugh at our jokes and they won't be afraid that something horrible is going to happen. On the contrary, it's Oscar Wilde. They'll know it's going to be hilarious. And even if they never find out what happens on account of our having mislaid Act Three, they won't mind. They'll forgive us. Think of that. They'll have been enjoying our company. A cultural experience. They'll have enjoyed us for what we are.

Kinsey Not who we are. Who we're dressed up and pretending to be. Lane the butler.

Allan Algernon.

Irene Gwendolen.

Rose Lady Bracknell.

George But that doesn't matter. That's the whole point. While we're standing here on this stage, that's who we are. If we do the play. Let me ask you, Allan. Who would you prefer to be? Algernon Moncrieff, wealthy bachelor with a flat in Half-Moon Street? Or Specs?

A pause

Kinsey And when it's over?

George It doesn't matter. It will have been a start.

A pause

George Specs?

Specs hurries off the stage

George There he is. He's back in the prompter's chair. He'll help us if things go wrong.

A pause. The others consider

Irene All right. Fuck it. Let's do it. But just get a move on this time.

Irene leaves. Kinsey glances at George, then follows

George, Rose and Allan are left on the stage as they were at the start

George Allan?

A pause

Allan I never had any control over anything I ever did. I'm not a bad
person, you know I'm not. But when certain things happen to you,
when they happen to you all your life, you're bound to explode. You
can't help it. But I was never in control. I told them that, but they
didn't believe me. Not then. Not now. Not ever.

George Specs will give you your cue.

Allan Will he?

George Yeah. He'll help you.

Allan (*resigned*) Right.

> *Allan leaves the stage*

Rose I feel nervous. Where are we going to begin?

George Back at the beginning. Where we were.

Rose Right.

George Do you want your line?

Rose No. I've got it.

A pause. Then the two of them return to character

Rose (*as Lady Bracknell*) Now to minor matters. Are your parents
living?

George (*as Jack Worthing*) I am afraid I really don't know. The fact is,
Lady Bracknell, I said I had lost my parents. It would be nearer the
truth to say that my parents have lost me … I don't actually know
who I am by birth. I was … well, I was found.

Rose (*as Lady Bracknell*) Found?

George (*as Jack Worthing*) The late Mr Thomas Cardew, an old gentleman of a very charitable and kindly disposition, found me, and gave
me the name of Worthing because he happened to have a first-class
ticket for Worthing in his pocket at the time. Worthing is a place in
Sussex: it is a seaside resort.

Rose (*as Lady Bracknell*) Where did the charitable gentleman, who
   had a first-class ticket for this seaside resort, find you?
George (*as Jack Worthing*) In a handbag.
Rose (*as Lady Bracknell*) A handbag?

The bell rings. An officious bell. The two of them freeze

*We hear slamming doors, locks turning. The grim sounds of a maximum
security installation. Nobody moves. Fade to Black-out*

THE END

FURNITURE AND PROPERTY LIST

On stage: Items at the director's discretion

Off stage: Ancient, hard-cover edition of the *The Importance of Being Earnest* with loose pages (**Specs**)

Personal: **Specs**: thick glasses

LIGHTING PLOT

Interior. The same scene throughout

To open: *General interior lighting*

Cue 1   Nobody moves
          Fade to black-out   (Page 33)

EFFECTS PLOT

Cue 1   **Allan** "Specs!"   (Page 12)
         Sound of a wedding march being played off stage on a
           xylophone

Cue 2   **George**: "The music stops."   (Page 12)
         Cut xylophone

Cue 3   **Rose** (*as Lady Bracknell*) "A handbag?"   (Page 33)
         Bell rings

Cue 4   **Rose** and **George** freeze   (Page 33)
         Doors slamming, locks turning

Printed by The Kingfisher Press, London NW10 7AS